My life in 21 poems

Lucindy Jordaan

BookLeaf Publishing

Presentation by *BookLeaf Publishing*

Web: www.bookleafpub.com

E-mail: info@bookleafpub.com

ISBN: 9789395756433

First edition 2022

DEDICATION

To Ryan, Lisa, Khloe and Emma, the reason I wake up every morning.

ACKNOWLEDGEMENT

Just before Covid took the world by storm, I discovered my life through counselling sessions with my wonderful counsellor. I learnt about my past, all the abuse and toxic behaviour I lived with. I had to make changes, an my counsellor saved my life.

PREFACE

Born as the 2nd child after my mother endured an infant loss. I was told they wanted me, the blessing...

But life was a rollercoaster of emotions and struggles, like many of us.

When I was a child

I grew up in that time
You know the one I say
When you see a child, that's fine
When you hear a child, that's nay

My memories are quite confined
My childhood seems so very bleak
My parents alcoholism was the big devide
Which makes my little life seem to reek

My father never spent time with us
My mother manipulate, abuse and controlled
Growing up quickly was the only plus
To forget my life in this household

My Brothers

I have two brothers
Younger than me
They were the favourite of my mother
For love I had to plea

The one is four years younger
My parents thought he did everything right
But that would be their ultimate blunder
After school he stayed out of sight

The other one is younger by a decade
Always the cute spoilt baby of the house
Living privately behind a friendly facade
Until the need for you arouse

14

This part carries a trigger for sexual abuse
Done by my step grandfather
At this age I was still a novice
No boyfriends or kisses I gathered

When I told my parents about this crime
I was told to forget and hide
Myself and me was now benign
And my heart broke in pieces and cried

I was not allowed to mention it
From thereon out, it affected my life
I wasn't worthy, so always submit
And my life was riddled with strife

My virginity

I went through life quiet and lonely
Too shy to live my life fully
Not a friend in sight I lived with closely
But a target for a close by bully

I set my values and morals quite high
To make me more worthy for love
But alas, my life was a big lonely sigh
The only love I knew was from above

I wanted to keep my virginity safe and sound
For the one who will turn my life around
But at a friends house with drinks and drugs
It was stolen at 20 and my heart unplugs

Lost

I got depressed and very lost
Feels like my life is going downhill
And my heart got frozen by Jack Frost
Who am I? What is God's will?

Nobody wants to be my one
My parents still don't care about me
My friends moved up in life, they won
But I am here, nothing to see

My happiness has long ago dried up
My worthlessness keeps increasing
My self-doubt has blown-up
My life is lost and hiding

1st Marriage

6

At work, I met this gentle bloke
And all my safety walls broke
He charmed me with his kindness
My heart were struck by blindness

He showed his true colours pretty soon
As soon as the honeymoon
And so continues my climbing worthlessness
I felt more lonely, I must confess

Luckily a good friend of mine
Helped me see this sign
17 months unhappily married
Finally free and this marriage was burried

The one

Nobody wants to be my one
The one who will love me just as I am
The one who will be my special someone
The one who's love for me is not a scam

The one who will make my life better
The one who will break down my walls
The one who will wrap me like a sweater
The one who will answer all my calls

The one who wants to be with me
The one who's heart I won
The one who is my tall steady tree
Nobody wants to be my one

2nd Marriage

8

After 3 years of a downhill slope
I met this much younger bloke
His smile so big it melts my heart
Not one day I want to be apart

Life threw it's big curve balls
And slowly but surely I put up my walls
We both are quite shy
We have no friends to live by

We struggled and moved forward
Life together was very awkward
We worked and we planned
To make our marriage stand

Ryan

After 2 years
Our son was born
The cutest little nose and ears
Our family of 3 was the norm

He has a hearing disability
But that does not stop him
He makes my life a reality
And I always believe in him

He is kind and caring
He is anxious and shy
His cuddles are repairing
My frozen heart in reply

Life as a mom

I love being a mother
and definitely want another
I don't mind not sleeping
It doesn't make me weeping

I love to see Ryan growing
I love to see him all knowing
Toddler time was getting hard
I make regular prayers to God

Being a mother just fits with me
No silent moment guarantee
Buying new things all the time
Life as a mother is sublime

Leaving South Africa

It has always been our plans
To immigrate to Australia abroad
With only our kids in our hands
As a brighter future we walk toward

Our bonds with our family was not strong
So wanting to go was an easy feat
In our lives nothing felt wrong
Our lives in South Africa was obsolete

It was easy leaving everything behind
It was exciting to start anew
A lost life refined
It wouldn't be easy, we knew

Life in Australia

With only a suitcase in hand
We left South-Africa and everyone
Everything just as we planned
It feels like we already won

Life was hard and we struggled
To pay to eat and survive
And our relationship was troubled
And a pregnancy for a family of five

Pregnancy went well
But my mental health suffered
As hubbies abuse excell
My love for him was smothered

Lisa

Lisa is my first princess in pink
And Ryan loved being a big brother
Life was going by in a blink
I loved to cuddle and touch her

She has a wonderful smile
And beautiful brown hair
And has her own style
And a heart full of care

She gets excited very quickly
My little social butterfly
And teething made her sickly
Lives life on high

Khloe

Khloe is my smallest bub
My 2nd princess, my blue eyed blonde
She lived in my arms, cosy and snug
Of me she is very fond

I think her life start off hard
As the yelling in the house escalate
And her little life is scarred
She finds her emotions hard to regulate

She is cute and petite
She has a very big heart
She makes my life complete
From me she doesn't want to part

The church of Jesus Christ of latter-day saints

We both grew up learning about Jesus
We both lived a kind quiet life
Knowing Jesus frees us
We have a lot of strife

Belong to a great community
It made life a lot easier
We no longer have a unit
Life become more and more messier

Living for God is my life
Living for Him makes me whole
I know I Was a good wife
And I need to take control

Emma

Just before I turned forty
I welcomed my little Emma, Big Girl
My little brown-eyed shortie
Who loves to cuddle and twirl

She found her place very quickly
Truly are the baby of the house
We are wrapped around her finger clearly
She rules us without a doubt

She is kind and caring
Sassy and daring
With a heart of gold
A true blessing I'm told

Turning 40

I do not feel like I should be forty
And I am definitely not naughty
I am quite overweight
At the moment life is not great

I feel completely unsupported
And I am beyond exhausted
Living with a partner who's toxic
Was a silent but true topic

I started with counselling
The things I learnt was astounding
To save my children and myself
I had to remove us from his shelf

Separation

I made a really difficult decision
In October 2020
It was a very easy transition
Thankfully we both parted friendly

For quite a while I was discombobulated
And going through various odd emotions
And dealing with them was complicated
But the light at the end, approaches

This decision was a really good one
Our lives improved and moved forward
Our new way of living has begun
Sometimes life can be a bit awkward

Lonliness

Day in and day out
Always the same
Brings loneliness about
And when I fail, the blame

My support group is scarce
In Australia no family
On me it puts a lot of stress
And my high anxiety increases rapidly

Living with anxiety is not easy either
Life with four children can be quite a task
And endless task without a breather
No one around to help out or ask

Single mom

Being a single mom is very draining
Just as much as it is rewarding
I spent a lot of time with my kids
A lot of laughs and also tears

Finding a job is very hard
When they are sick it's up to my part
I wish I can find time to look after me
Everyone says that is the key

But when, when can I find time
To take care of me and be fine
But days without them is a bore
I have to be with them for evermore

Blessings

Looking at how far I come
I learnt to accept myself as a wonderful mum
Ryan is a big brother teen
Loving us dearly, no inbetween

Lisa is my first girl preteen
Like a wonderful acquired cuisine
Khloe is my special one
With lots of laughter and fun

Emma is my youngest child
Lots of cuddles and a little bit wild
True blessings in this poem of last
All my dreams have surpassed